A Strange
Catechism

A Strange
Catechism

Poems

Carol,
I look forward to more conversations once dinner is prepared.
Every blessing and in gratitude

Justen Ahren

Copyright © 2013 by Justen Ahren.

Library of Congress Control Number: 2013910644
ISBN: Hardcover   978-1-4836-5394-5
             Softcover   978-1-4836-5393-8
             Ebook   978-1-4836-5395-2

All rights reserved. No part of this book may be reproduced or transmitted in any form or by any means, electronic or mechanical, including photocopying, recording, or by any information storage and retrieval system, without permission in writing from the copyright owner.

This book was printed in the United States of America.

First Edition

Rev. date: 06/20/2013

To order additional copies of this book, contact:
Xlibris Corporation
1-888-795-4274
www.Xlibris.com
Orders@Xlibris.com
134884

Contents

Acknowledgments 9

I.

What Cannot Be Said Is Wept

Molt 13
After Birth, a Dream of Weight 14
After Birth 16
Resurrect 17
Annunciation 18
Ascension 19
Aubade 20
Shrive 21
Barbed Wire 22

II.

The Bells in Her Mouth Are Ringing

Weather 25
The Bells in Her Mouth 26
Catechism 28
Vigil 30
Coatesville, Pennsylvania 31
Gone 32
Night 33
Confirmation 34
Absence 35
Photograph 36

Found	37
Cherry Tree	38
Counting Backward	39
Route 41	41
Pruning	42
While I Was Sleeping	43

III.

A Strange Catechism

A Strange Catechism	47
Matins	48
Crawl inside the Trees to Sleep	49
Vesper	50
Matins	51
Sunrise	52
Vesper	53
Independence Day	54
Matins	55
Vesper	56
Among the Roots of an Old Tree	57
Alter	58
Vesper	59
Communion	60
Vesper	61
Discharged	62
Parking Lot with Starlings	63
Gone Quiet	64
Creek at the Sea's Door	65
Penance	67

To those who have lost children
And to children who have lost childhood

For David and for Lucas

Acknowledgments

Grateful acknowledgments to the following:

The editors of the journals in which these poems first appeared: *Fulcrum: An Annual of Poetry and Aesthetics, The Comstock Review, Borderlands: Texas Poetry Review,* and *BorderSenses.*

My friends and the faculty at the San Miguel Poetry Week, where many of these poems were nurtured and improved.

Jorie Graham, Honor Moore, and Jennifer Tseng for their careful reading and feedback.

Rob Berkeley, thanks for insisting upon this book's publication and for challenging me to write every day.

Dr. Marianne Goldberg and the Pathways Projects Initiative for their continual support of my work and for helping to make this book a reality.

Deborah and David Brown, thanks for your generous contribution that made publication possible and inevitable.

Traeger di Pietro for creating, on demand, the painting *The Bells in Her Mouth,* for the cover.

My wife, Sara Ahren, who provides me with time and space—a luxury while raising two kids—in order to write, which she understands I must do. I love you.

In gratitude.

I.

What Cannot Be Said Is Wept

Molt

When a soul is ready, it sheds its ghost skin, takes off
its clear feathers like a rain. The doctors examine

and prescribe to my body, but no one says *Grieve*
until the heart's faulty core, hung in curtains, can be rebuilt.

Nothing they give me fills the hole. Still my mind holds
every dream I had for you. An entire house prepared.

The tiles on the floor are cold. The hallway
of the maternity wing is fluorescent and cold. I am afraid

nothing else will happen. I won't die of this.
I'll just go on walking in the numb past, missing you,

sitting in the chair by the window, knees curled up,
waiting for that one bird I grew inside to release his song.

After Birth, a Dream of Weight

i.

What color were his eyes?
What color was his hair?
I can't remember.
The mud-filled rain we were
together in a dream. The dirt-
heavy boot of the moon sinking
in its dark sanctuary of the mind.
Child, my child briefly in my arms,
I dream of the way
we were before separate.

ii.

The nurse wakes me.
Are you all right? she asks.
The stars behind the trees are out.
You didn't let me hold him, I say.
What color were his eyes?
Why couldn't I hold him?
before you took him
to fill with tubes
and weigh his brief life.

iii.

Through the first cold night, I shook.

Alone in the house's shadow.

And the oaks leaned together in the wind.

I did not eat.

Without him I could not sleep.

Then one day,

as on any other day, the sun rose.

A red leaf,

my heart, fell to ice.

After Birth

I want the weight of you,
your body, bush of yellowbird song,
the frail connection I sang to
each morning you were
within me, fusing to *if,*
is, perhaps.
I call your name. Now
the doctors give me something.
For the pain, they say.

If I stop returning to your memory,
stop filling this room with breath,
you will vanish. From my arms,
you will vanish. A language of leaves,
a language of wings,
then nothing will be left
to lend me your shape.

Resurrect

I can make a bird out of you, out of sticks,
keep you in a vessel I can blow into and fill with breath,
then, in the condensation, write your name and kiss it.

Last night, I had the strength to dream you.
You become a swallow. You sing in the eaves,
and I feel almost whole. But I cannot swallow you,

take you down into the windowless room within me—
your hands and feet pressing out again, your body surging
beneath my surface. You sing until dusk and then fly off.

In the hospital, I remember hearing your heart's murmur,
whistling through the tiny hole in me. Someday, it will matter
that everything continues to happen—the hollowness too.

The dogs bark after you're gone. A nest remains, impossibly
empty, born of the beams of the house.

Annunciation

Night coming, cold coming early
to the photo I keep inside.

The doctors tell me you are gone.
They lie. I see you

as I see the road
veering, the rail

see, the yellow-black
arrows, see above,

sun twisted
in trees.

I don't want a ghost,
just the stirring of birds

you were within me
day and night.

Ascension

When I tell them I see you lift from the branch
above the creek, a feathered thing, they don't believe me.
Though I tell them your mouth is perfect, they say, *Shhh.*

Though I'm laughing, *It is him,* and my fingers are trembling
toward you, encouraging you to fly closer so I can hold you,
and they will see. But you are gone. My faint voice goes

after you, asking the nurses who hold and sedate me
if they see the child the bird. *Lie down,* they say.
There is no bird. Come. Away from the windows.

They leave me a stark, deformed heaven.
They leave me a tattered nest you won't return to—
the bells in my mouth ringing.

Aubade

Snow mantles the oak
limbs twisted by wind, soil.

Paw prints in it betray the cat
lurking beneath the bush.

Beyond the shadow of the house,
it melts. Robins hunt in the mud.

I've turned back the cold,
daffodils unstoppable, sun's coming.

This morning, I leave again, and I'm left
with the memory of your body: how

soft it fell, covering me, an instant
when you were all I was.

Shrive

> *I can't tell if the day is ending, or the world.*
> —Anna Akhmatova

You turn me to rain with a sentence.
Black and secret centers have me falling,
confessing I know nothing but the crusts of words,
the starvation we call living.
All day the earth broke open.
Under a furrowed brow of clouds,
crows rose, smoke, and thin crocuses.

Barbed Wire

When I told him I was pregnant,
he filled the tub with hot water,

forced me to sit in it,
drinking a tea of bitter herbs.

When I kept you, he left.
I nursed you on tears

shed all winter. The moon
in the window turned

my body blue like snow at night.
Hand on the macadam of my belly,

I felt for you, my child,
tumbling beneath.

The night you were born, it snowed,
wind blew, closed the roads. I imagined

your father crossing the fields he'd known
his whole life, following

the staggered line of fence posts
tied to cords of barbed wire.

II.

The Bells in Her Mouth

Are Ringing

Weather

February 1976.
It is raining.
I'm watching my mother
walk barefoot in the litter
and the broken bottles
along the shoulder of the road.
I'm watching the sky
drag yellow clouds of slag.
She punches at
the wind, her mouth
ringing open, startling
the unseen, screaming
at the birds. At the trees.
She is cursing.

The Bells in Her Mouth

i.

We went stomping around in an Easter rain,
looking for the plot. I laid flowers on
my brother's unmarked grave.

Afterward, in the churchyard,
a boy from school called me the name
my mother had used: *retarded.*

I leaped on his back, punching,
and stuffed his mouth with mud
then dragged him through the privet.

My mother said, washing out the cuts,
tears fell from the blue sleeves of the statue
of Our Lady of Consolation.

ii.

A miracle, she told me.
My brother had appeared to her
at birth, luminous, and perfect.

But the nurses shunted him away
and filled him with tubes.

Too deformed to swallow,
they told her. His mouth was
a hole. He could not eat.

A Strange Catechism

iii.

She locked herself in her bedroom.
After supper—a bowl of Lucky Charms—
I went to her with a nest the swallows

started above the door, with cuttings
from the forsythia she beat back
from the windows year after year.

Do not eat of this world,
she warned as I left,
unless you are willing to suffer.

Catechism

We are leaving.
In the snow, we are leaving

footprints on the sidewalk. We are going
with our suitcases. We are going

to pray in the blue light of the church.
Hurrying under leafless trees, I count

birds preening in their battered
nests—high up toward the wind—

at their stations. As we walk,
my hand warms in my mother's.

Her arms are so thin, they look like my own.
From the last pew, I watch as she washes

the feet of the statues of certain saints,
bowing low in her whispering,

pressing them for protection
as they protect scrap

metal and furnaces, slag
heaps, and wood-handled shovels.

I watch as she lights a candle for the one
she no longer speaks of,

then she drags me out again beneath the dark limbs.
What are we running from?

From the sky, snow continues
quietly, covering our tracks.

Or is it ash that is falling on the birds
now sleeping?

And where are we going to sleep?
Where are we going?

Vigil

Her footprints in the snow, I follow
past the statues of angels, find her

coat where she left it lying
by his grave. I need her too.

When the lights go out,
the moon begins searching

for those who lit candles,
for the recently orphaned.

We shared bread on the low steps
of the church, where a radio plays

war—the first bombs already falling.
And when she falls, tired of yelling,

when her body gathers cold,
turning sky, guns, bombs, turning blue,

I find the marks
in the snow his twin wings

left beside her, brushing the earth.
Rest, be quiet, be still, she says.

*We are alone. The whole
damned world's skidding on.*

COATESVILLE, PENNSYLVANIA

Black rectangles like coffins
laid out along the Brandywine.

Silver lunch pails went in, cigarettes
and jeans. Yellow hard hats went in.

The lines of men we looked after.
I know the names of the dead

we pass on the way to Sunday
dinner. Their graves stare at me

across the shallow valley,
down our street of leafless oaks.

At night—steel plates clanging
blast furnace—firing orange

against the lead sky—the slag
train moving deep beside the river

wakes me. It is here
I begin to hope I'll die in my sleep.

Gone

To that strange flower, absence.
Each day begins with birds
singing, and the rain is appropriate,
running through the cracks in reality.

Do you know where I go when I leave you? she asks.

She coughs. The air is poisoning her.
She walks through town, yelling at me, *Keep up!*
I fear her going.
She hides in the closets of the house while I search.
She licks dew from rocks
and crawls inside the trees to sleep.
It rains up.

She says, *You are afraid to love me.*

Night

Night came, sirens.

Dark and breathless, it came

with the limp shape of my mother in its arms.

In its white coat, it came with her from the bath

laid her on the floor in the hall.

It struck her blue mouth

forced the metal of its own mouth over the water of hers.

It blew into her again

and again. It said, *Stay.*

It asked her name.

Morning came.

Tender it came

as tender as the one before.

It brought walls

and the doors of the house stood

swinging open and closing upon our secrets

for everyone to see. For days,

I slept with the words

I'd heard her singing in the tub

Hello, darkness.

Confirmation

Held my breath until morning

vomited. The more luminous

the day, the less definite

I become. I began

by going out beyond the edge of her

body's shadow. Felt

the effect of words: how small

I was made—a starvation

kneading the air she put God in.

Absence

She left a photo of herself
for me to kiss at night

some crayons
and coloring books

but what will I eat?
While she's gone

the house searches for her shape.

To be inside her breath
and warm beneath the covers

I draw trees
in the yard of a house

I once knew. My fingers
keep making them

in the air
until dawn.

Photograph

In it, I can hear the wind,
the charcoal of the place burning.

The dust of me in the yard,
unsettling the ants,

lighting matches, and dropping them
into their holes. The clothes

left hanging on the line
want you. I want you. Your skin

inside those shirts, which, like the days,
have grown entwined.

Before bed, I kiss the picture.
It's not like having her here

sitting by the window,
blowing on the window,

drawing in the wet circle
of her breath his name,

shadow of another good-bye.

Found

They found her after
three days, in the parking lot,
standing, turning counter-
clockwise in a circle,
her fingers wound
together like roots
of old trees, holding
a bundle of his clothes.

When I picture her,
she is not like this.
She is holding a nest.
She is kneeling beside
the sink, crying,
*You shouldn't have to see me
like this.* I take her
sadness, and I swallow it.

CHERRY TREE

The cherry is leaking amber sap,

trapping the bees that happen upon the bark.

She stares out the window mostly

since she's been home. I'm afraid to disturb her.

Outside of her room, I pause

with breakfast on a tray. Hearing her stir within,

I enter without knocking and see the scars

on her wrists—the naked raised chains of attempts.

A late frost bruises the cherry blossoms.

In the yard, a cessation of bees.

Counting Backward

Three months, and no one I love has left
in the middle of the night, been taken
and not returned, broken
their promise, disappeared.
I am eating again, crusts,
and praying to the birds—their hollow
bones, their rapid hearts,
beating words and stories. Of the past,
I can say there were days
when I spoke to no one.
I befriended trees, rocks,
and the rocks in the creek.
When my mother returns,
it won't be long
until we leave.

In pajamas, I've left, in the snow,
after punching a man in the nuts,
after tearing a cross from his neck
for pulling her hair.
I am ten, and I can start a car,
lock the doors when she tells me to.

I can talk about my penny collection

while she steals

from the pockets of her boyfriend's jeans.

On the floor, by the bed,

I can lie quietly while she apologizes

with her body. I can stay quiet for days

in the new shape of a place

until she's feeling better. I can count backward

from twenty-nine the places we've slept.

Route 41

I've returned many times to look at things
no one else will notice—the two dull lanes

of asphalt cutting through corn-stubble fields,
the aluminum trailer on the side of the road,

propped on blocks and rocked by trucks,
rolling south through the gray steel mornings.

There is the diner where my father sat.
In the corner of the parking lot, the blue-and-

-silver phone booth. It is not extraordinary,
except this is the phone he called from,

telling her he wasn't coming home. Disappearing
is how he says good-bye. Inside the booth, hinged

door shut, I lift the phone from its cradle. Listen.
Maybe it was as my mother said: I cried too much.

Pruning

Working from the newest growth back,
I come to the healed scars, the past
cuts my mother made circling these bushes
in her patched jeans. How did she choose?

Alone in the damp March fog before crocuses,
it is difficult to believe anything will come
from these twisted branches, let alone sweet,
blue berries that snap open in the mouth.

Without encouragement, without embrace,
I prune as she taught, sacrificing the weak,
diseased branches that won't amount to much.
I cut and let them drop and, as I do,

remember the feeble bull she tended
twice a day, turning him on a bed of straw
with the blanket-padded bucket of the tractor
and, too, the quiet boy who stretched her sweater,

afraid to disturb her and who grew forgotten
like the corners of her house. How is it she decided
she could live without a thing long loved
and carried in her dreams through winter?

While I Was Sleeping

In the parking lot, a dog suckles a pig.
A black cat is dead on the red tile roof.

The bells of the churches ring
out of sync. An uncertain evening,

our time together, and much is past.
Where did you go while I was sleeping?

Birds grew no wings. Snow wet
the oak boughs, or were they black from ash?

At the edge of town, the creek searched
for the sea. You never told me

it would catch fire, poisoning the air
with smoke. With slender arms,

you used to embrace me, saying nothing.
Where did you go while I was sleeping?

Birds grew no wings, didn't circle
this evening the cathedral of your face,

the seal of your lips. Can you hear me?
Am I nothing?

III.
A Strange Catechism

A Strange Catechism

I can't talk about the fog
in my body, the nest
made of paper and tattered
leaves, the collection of
shiny things my mouth attracts.
Could it be I need only
say your name to receive
the fluttering of light that rises
to my window, a memory
of that dream that lent me your shape?
I feel inside a strange catechism
has begun, learning down the sound
of my love for God
into the dark of my body.

Matins

Transcribe mourning doves' songs,
chronicle the ants' warring
over little mounds, choreograph
the leaves in the fingers of wind,
coax them to stretch and lean
like cats, perform the fly's ablutions

Crawl Inside the Trees to Sleep

The souls from which
atmosphere is fashioned appear,
project their stories on screens
of air, their little houses, this dirty valley,
showing me how they live. Some are poor.
Their homes with crooked windows sit
on little turns in the creek with fields and rows
of gardens going out from them.
Some sit removed, alone among spruce
or in hollows where chained dogs bark
at the mud and drizzle. I see them huddled
by the gates of the mills, mowed down
by teams of beasts and men
harnessed to machines, and finally, robotically,
how they were wagered and traded and sold
as ballast on seafaring vessels, and shoveled
into furnaces. But some grow doors
in their chests at this time, portals
in their hearts to safe havens, closets
with deep interiors and lovely dresses,
where they hide from the Great Impatience
rifling the world's house.

Vesper

Pause in the evening

Where do I fit prayers?

In my body many names

I've called, and still I've nothing

worth giving the square shape of God

MATINS

On the edge of morning
I anchor my feet to the cold
tile floor. Maples' filter through
fog. Shadows fall
across the unmade bed. I am
without strings, without angels

Sunrise

The woman gesturing obscenely at the intersection
of First and Main—who sleeps on a bench
in the cemetery or in the doorway of the church,

her blankets covered in bird melodies—is responsible
for this morning's frost. And the clouds
skirting the orange sky were dragged here

by the man pulling a shopping cart full of empty
bottles down the alley to his house. Someone shits
in the street, and snowdrops break through the ground.

I'd like to meet the man who makes the sun rise
and the person who lifts the tide, laundering the earth.
They must be strong. Water is so heavy

and reluctant, it must be a mother in the barrio,
carrying her feverish child upstairs to bed.
And keeping the cooking flame lit, there

where there is no food, two lovers in a field
of sheets. What a gift they are giving—
their forgiveness of each another, bringing rain.

Vesper

This evening, the sky's salt
the *golodrinas* alight in
the hydrangeas' blue clouds
a gray mouse scurries under
the world without me
may be the real one

Independence Day

A plume of black smoke rises to the north of the city.
A woman runs the streets, her hair coming loose,
screaming about an army in beards lynching.

My mind collapses, a plume of black smoke.
White birds scatter from a leafed-out tree
that blooms for the first time anyone can remember—

red candle-like flowers setting fire to the town square.
Artists scamper into trees and onto rooftops
to sketch the edge of the world coming

before any of us can fathom it from the street.
Dressed in a nightgown and skin washed with lilac
water, made sweet for this day, I awaken into

the deeper dream. All I've seen behind my eyes pales.
The ragged army drags its rusty cannon into town,
stealing our chickens and bread and shoes. If I can love

each of these men into the canopy's fireworks
of sunlight and moths circling, love them
in the dandelions, then send them away full of gravy

and the drowsy scent of me on their cheeks, this violence
will go no farther than my street. My body
be their confessional. Touch the dark grains of me,

lay your heads upon my screen, you lost children of god.
All you've destroyed will be given to you gladly, in the deeper
dream we call awake, if only you find the courage to ask.

Matins

I held you in the parking lot
What made what beat there
between us, collecting rain?
God the shape mind makes dreaming
eyes close here open there—
in the apron of my skirt nectarines

VESPER

What do I think?
You are never far
and the air isn't cruel here
only different. But is it
that I think of you near me
that makes it cruel?

Among the Roots of an Old Tree

I found the tendrils of your fingers
wound around mine like prayers,

woven into the clothing of prayer,
and fled with you in my arms,

along the highway of snakes,
hiding you from the streetlights

and stars, from dogs barking down alleys.
Nothing should speak of this.

No one would believe—
they'd shut me away again

in a room with no views.
I went without words, with you

in a bundle, and took you out in the cold
stone light of the chapel to discover

the strange grasp memory had exhumed—
at last what I'd sung to by candlelight

had returned to me, living, a shadow
beating its wings against the wall,

gathering in the corner, scattering
the shells of acorns I'd eaten through.

Alter

The night you were born,
the moon in the window
turned my body blue
like snow at night. Hand
on the macadam of my belly,
I felt you moving
as a wave in the dark.

I am grateful.
I am fastening words,
fashioning stories. I am beginning
again. Today is February.
A plastic bag
caught on barbed wire
flutters in the wind.

No, let me begin again.
Morning, a red leaf,
fingers free from ice.

Vesper

Those who have lost children
find in repeating their names
music after a while in the soul's
missing, they no longer float away
without the lead of accompaniment
someone is always singing
in the evening, lighting candles
and the sparrows come

Communion

The mouth of the priest visits
this morning, smudging

the sky, promising me
fewer things

than coal-laced
January rain

like small pills
the nurses bring

in paper cups on a silver tray
each morning, the dull

communion.
He tells me to swallow

the immaculate
name of my holy mother

ten times. He says,
You will not be forgiven.

Here, some water.
The mouth of the priest visits

smudging this morning.
The sky.

Vesper

God, you do not love
a filthy child
bringing you selfish prayers
Look at my hands
dirty from rooting
Am I not good enough
to stand before the dent of your body?

Discharged

I blow prayers into my fingers
to warm them while I wait,
but no one comes for me.
I say your name, and I drift
like paper through the empty lot.
Where is that answer now, the sun?
My mouth is an abandoned nest.
In the broken bells,
ribbon, and insulation.
On my wrist a bracelet with a name.
It is something.

Parking Lot with Starlings

Turning counterclockwise
in the parking lot beneath the lamppost,
he visits me. This is how
I find him, where I feel him residing
inside me again, upside down.
From the sky, brown drizzle,
some warmth I can recognize. Above
the barren earth, a murmuration—numinous
starlings twine and
don't stop to gather joy.

Gone Quiet

The last hydrangea flowers in the cold
autumn morning continuing after
happiness is happiness no longer.
In my housecoat, in the window, I watch,
the pollen-dusted faces of the bees
a pane's distance from my hunger.
And just as I'm prepared to let go,
the blue flowers whispering draw me back down
toward the same collision the bees are steered.
All of my stinging, alone in the night,
calling to you from the darkness of known things,
is gone, leaving me stunned in the quiet.

CREEK AT THE SEA'S DOOR

I remember missing the limbs of trees
I crawled beneath to sleep in their yellow
leaves and birdsongs. You knocked at the door,
you found me, flowing out the blue minutes
from cuts made on my body. You carried
me from bed, out in the rain, growing wild.

When he left, I was desperate, wild,
barely sleeping, and eating at the trees'
roots, holding on to the banks. I carried
no music. The sun was only yellow
while I sought his figure. There were minutes,
I believed he waited just beyond the door.

Where my story ends, yours begins. Your door
next to mine, you must have heard me call, wild
for him to stay, hold him a few minutes—
the winged ghost I'd been chasing through the trees.
Following it for days in the yellow
canopy it flew through, his song carried

me forward one more day. While you carried
on your silent vigil outside my door,
peeking through the keyhole, letting yellow
morning light in through the blinds, his wild
chorus grew dimmer in the molting trees.
I'd lost you both, my children, but minutes.

I missed you growing up, missed the minute
details. So deep was the grief I carried
after your brother died. I crawled home to the trees
that stretched their safety over my door.
I'd rest, and you could too. Without my wild
migrations, you might find the yellow

apron of a mother's love. But yellow
evenings alone, I grew restless. Minutes
alone in the flat of my mind turned me wild
again. I sought the channels that carried
grief from my body to that distant door.
The nurse says I'm lucky I was found. The trees

in the valley have turned yellow. The minutes
are crying from the trees, giving to the wild, tear-
fed creek—love's prayers to carry to the sea's door.

Penance

Get dressed

Scrape the dirt from beneath my nails

Sweep evil from the porch

Laugh with the fluorescent soul of my son

Scream into a jar

Gather the apples that have fallen to the grass

Make supper

Let the evening cold-driven wasp in

That beats its papery body against the window

Two swallows fold in the air

like two hands taking in the laundry

The warmth I can give, I must give it

Edwards Brothers Malloy
Thorofare, NJ USA
July 9, 2013